Air Power

MIKOYAN MiG-35

MEGAN COOLEY PETERSON

BLACK RABBIT BOOKS

Bolt is published by Black Rabbit Books
P.O. Box 3263, Mankato, Minnesota, 56002.
www.blackrabbitbooks.com

Jennifer Besel, editor; Grant Gould & Michael Sellner, designers; Omay Ayres, photo researcher

Library of Congress Cataloging-in-Publication Data
Names: Peterson, Megan Cooley, author.
Title: Mikoyan MiG-35 / by Megan Cooley Peterson.
Description: Mankato, Minnesota : Black Rabbit Books, [2019] | Series: Bolt. Air power | Includes bibliographical references and index. | Audience: Grades 4-6. | Audience: Ages 9-12.
Identifiers: LCCN 2017026469 (print) | LCCN 2017027692 (ebook) | ISBN 9781680725018 (ebook) | ISBN 9781680723854 (library binding) | ISBN 9781680726794(paperback)
Subjects: LCSH: MiG (Fighter planes)—Juvenile literature.
Classification: LCC UG1242.F5 (ebook) | LCC UG1242.F5 P4736 2019 (print) | DDC 358.4/383—dc23
LC record available at https://lccn.loc.gov/2017026469

Printed in China. 3/18

Image Credits

acecombat.wikia.com: Dmitri Teekhov, 16-17; af.mil: Master Sgt. Mark C. Olsen, 19 (t); Staff Sgt. Andrew Lee, 25 (t); Alamy: ITAR-TASS Photo Agency, 13 (t); ITAR-TASS Photo Agency, 22–23, 26 (r); SPUTNIK, 1; chaspikserial.ru/: Cover; commons.wikimedia.org: Anatoly, 28-29; Sean Silva, 4–5; Dreamstime: Artyomanikeev, 13 (b); en.wikipedia.org: FFA P-16, 14-15; Nockson, 6; Ralf Roletschek, 25 (b); Getty: Kommersant Photo, 26 (l); navy.mil: Mass Communication Specialist 2nd Class Michael B. Zingaro, 19 (b); rusplane.ru: Yuri in, 3, 20–21; Shutterstock: A.S.B., 8–9; inspired-fiona, 15 (bkgd); Kisov Boris, 32; Meoita, 31; piscari, 18; sr.wikipedia.org: High Contrast_Reload, 27; the-blueprints.com/: 12 (t), 12–13 (bkgd); vectorthrust.wikia.com: 12 (b)
Every effort has been made to contact copyright holders for material reproduced in this book. Any omissions will be rectified in subsequent printings if notice is given to the publisher.

CONTENTS

CHAPTER 1

SPREADING Its Wings

It was a cloudy day in early 2017. A crowd gathered near Moscow, Russia. The MiG-35's engines thundered as it soared overhead. All eyes were on the sky. For the first time, a big audience saw this plane fly.

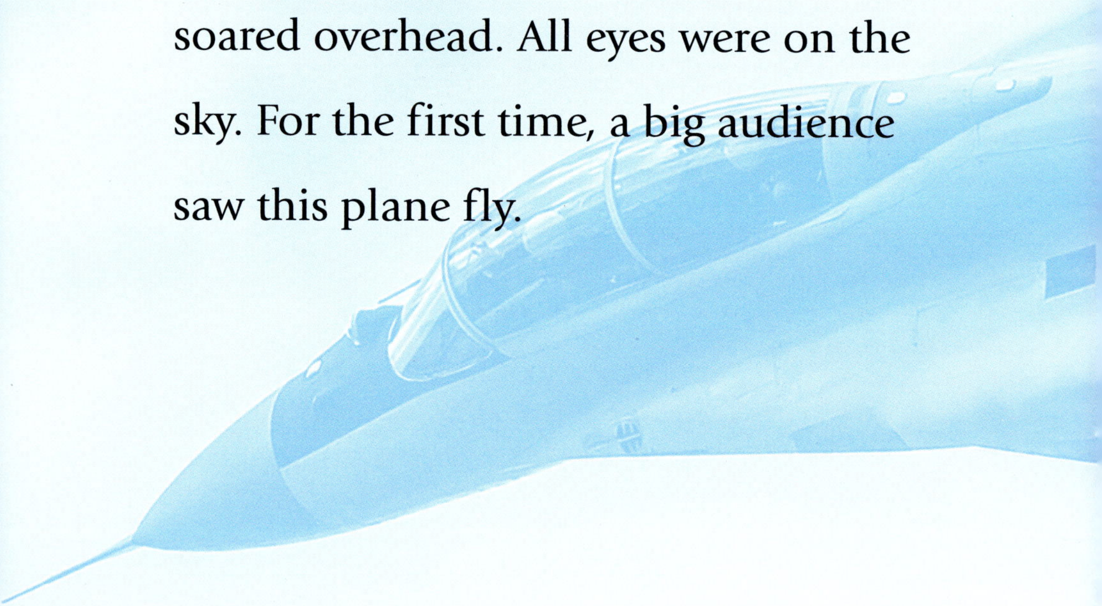

A Winning Flight

The pilot showed off the new fighter jet. He zoomed at a low **altitude**. He flew **barrel rolls**. The pilot called the plane a pleasure to fly.

The MiG-35's test flight lasted about eight minutes.

CHAPTER 2

HISTORY of the MiG-35

The Russian Air Force has flown Mikoyan MiG fighters since the 1940s. MiGs are fast, deadly fighters. The MiG-35 is the newest Russian jet. It has powerful speeds and weapons.

During the Korean War (1950–1953), Russian pilots flew MiG-15s. These feared fighters took down U.S. bomber planes.

Upgrades

Like MiGs before it, the 35 has a smooth body shape. But the MiG-35 has many upgrades. Engineers improved the **radar**. They also gave it a system that aims weapons. Enemies can't **detect** this system. They won't know if the MiG is firing at them.

TIMELINE OF THE MiG-35

Early 2000s

Engineers design the MiG-35.

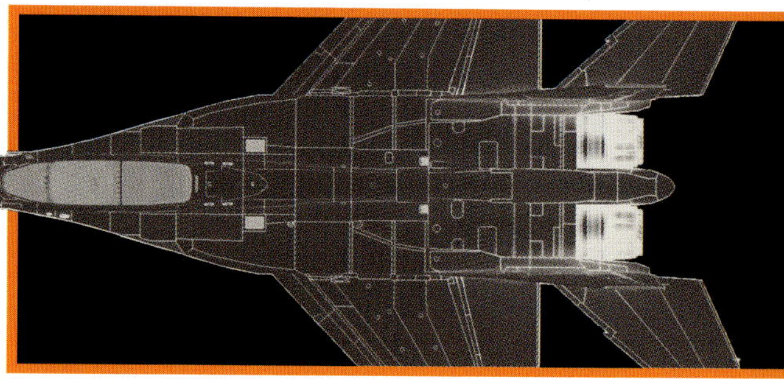

1935

1940

first MiG fighters produced

2007
shown to the public for first time

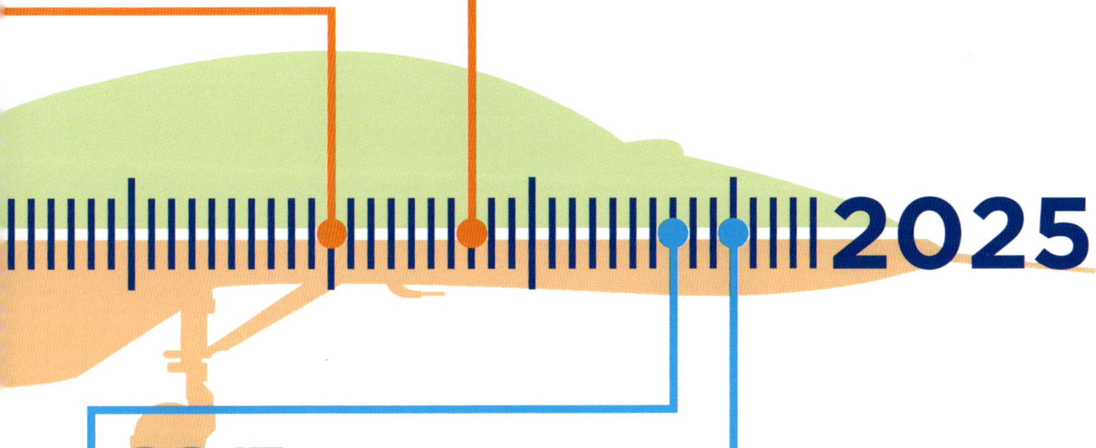

2017
enters test flights

by 2020
expected to be combat ready

CHAPTER 3

MiG-35 FEATURES

The MiG-35 is built for speed. It can fly more than 1,600 miles (2,575 kilometers) per hour. That's faster than most other fighter jets.

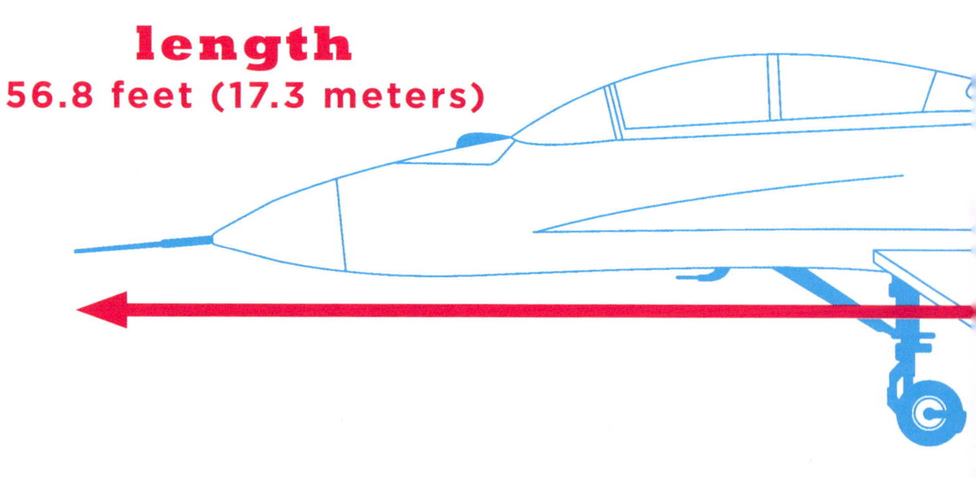

MiG-35 STATS

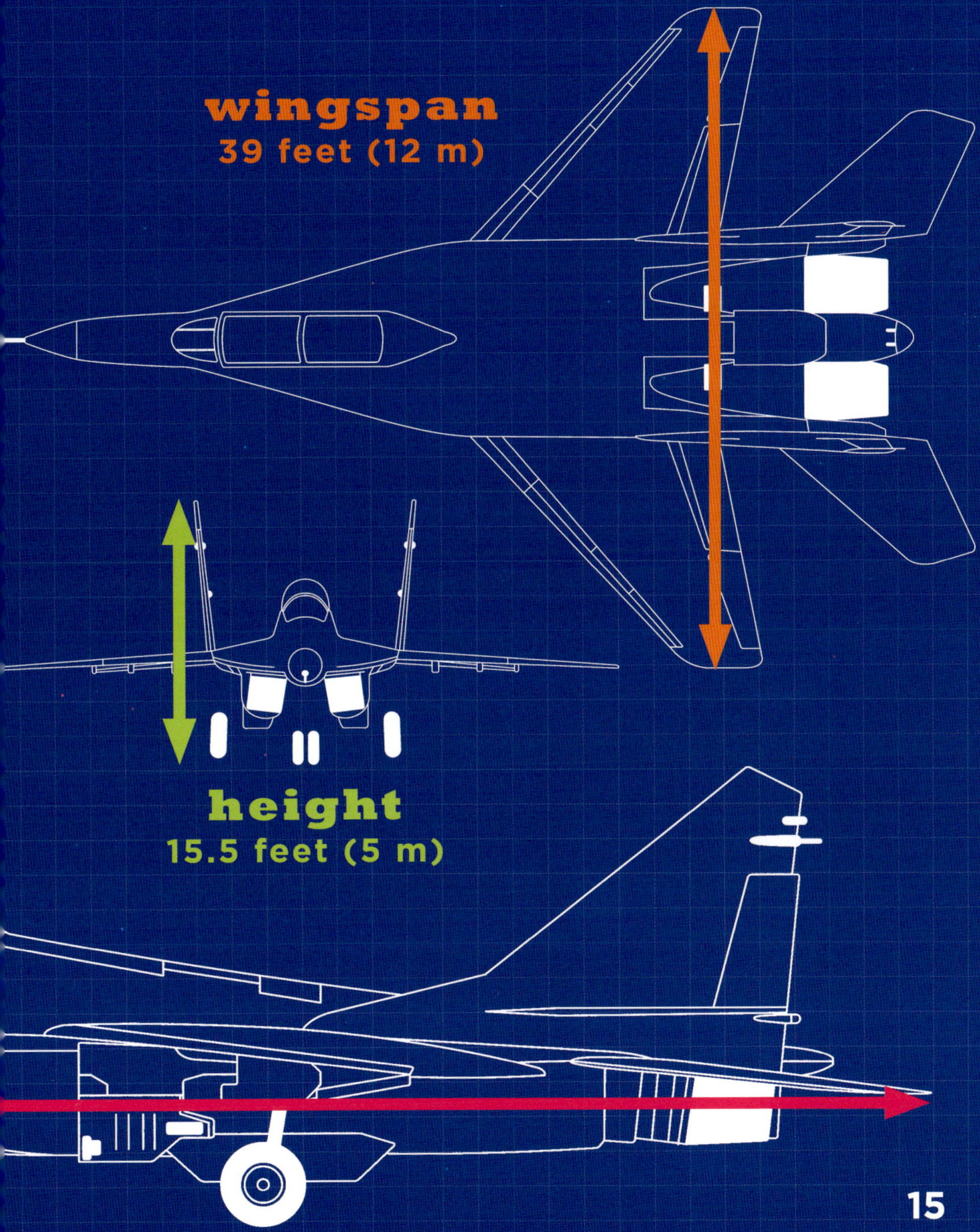

The MiG-35 has an extra fuel tank for use on long missions.

Weapons Load

The MiG-35 carries many weapons. It has a 30-mm **cannon**. It also carries **missiles** and bombs. These weapons attack air and ground targets.

High-Tech Radar

High-tech radar is one of the MiG-35's greatest tools. An antenna on the jet's nose sends and receives information. It tracks targets over land and sea.

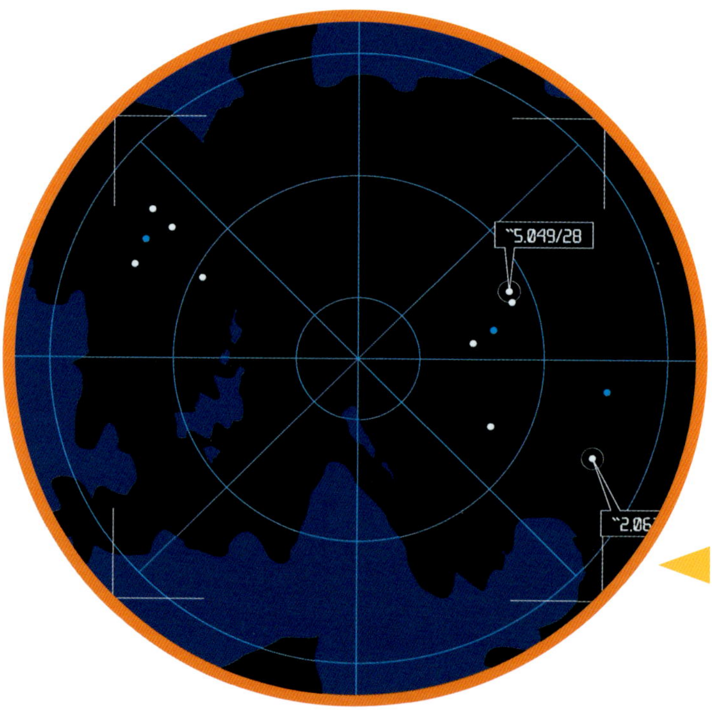

Finding Targets

spots aircraft
99 miles
(160 km) away

spots ships
186 miles
(300 km) away

tracks up to
30 targets at once

Experts think systems on the MiG-35 can spot stealth planes.

Crew

This fighter seats one or two pilots. The two-seat planes might be used for training. Onboard computers help pilots fly the jets.

MiG-35 PARTS

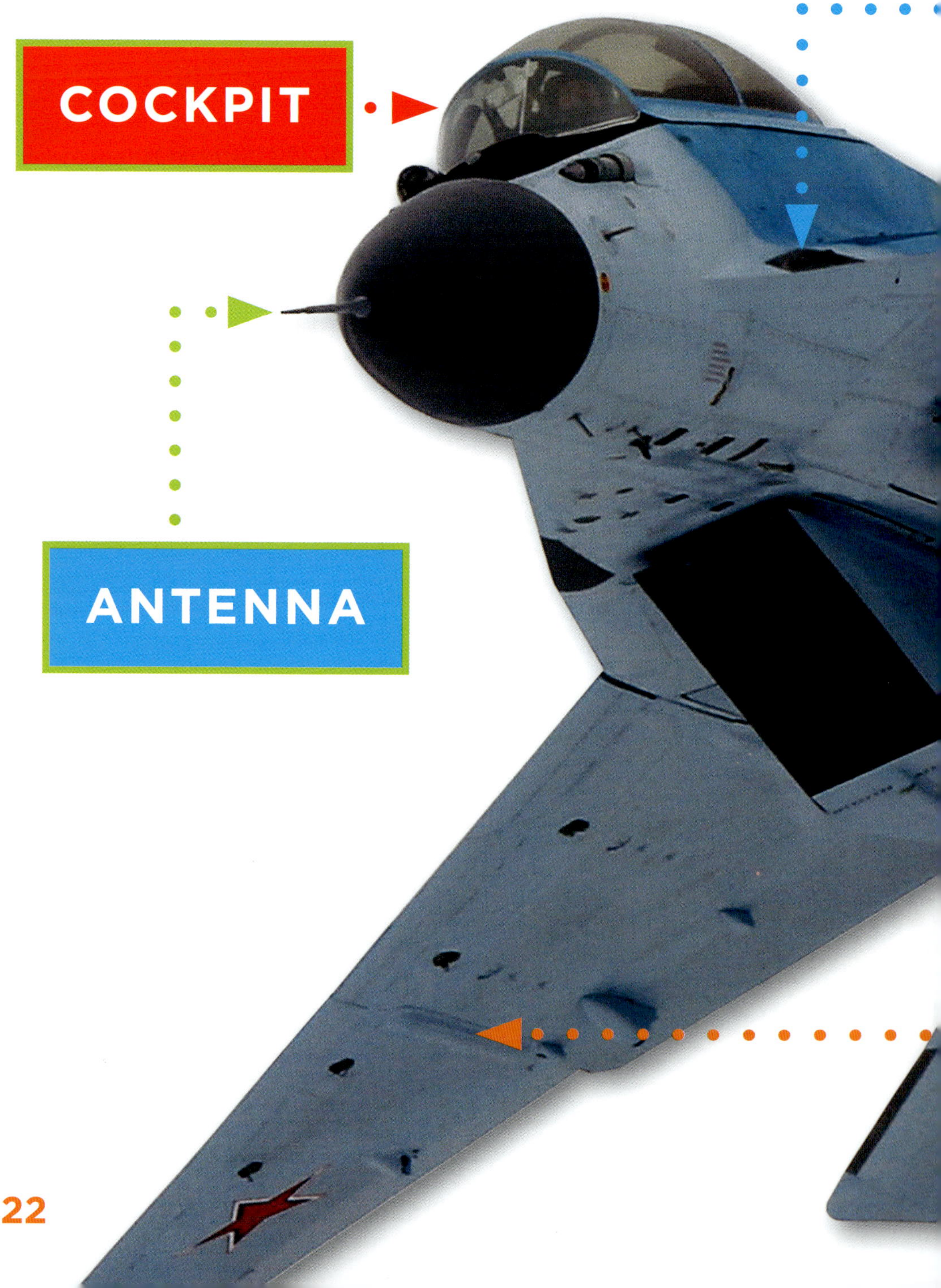

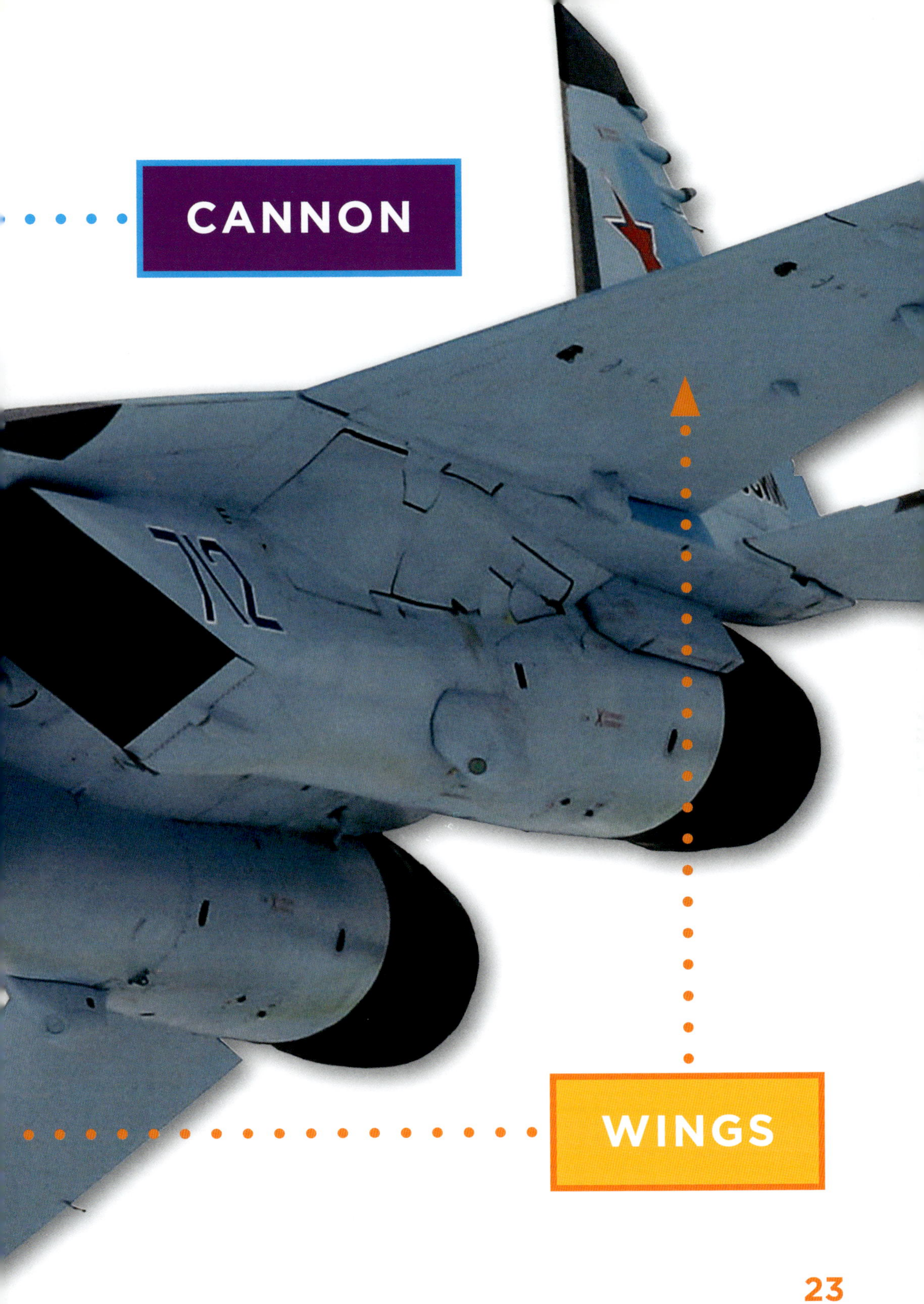
CANNON
WINGS

CHAPTER 4

The MiG-35 in ACTION

The MiG-35 does not have the stealth of some fighters. But it can zip in and out of turns quickly. The MiG-35 is a real threat in a **dogfight**.

Russia's Mikoyan MiG-35	vs.	United States' F-35A Lightning II
$15,600	flight cost per hour	$43,200
more than 1,600 miles (2,575 km) per hour	top speed	1,200 miles (1,931 km) per hour
1,926 miles (3,100 km)	range	1,381 miles (2,223 km)

BY THE NUMBERS

2

NUMBER OF ENGINES

$55 million

COST TO BUILD

65,477 POUNDS
(29,700 kilograms)
MAXIMUM TAKEOFF WEIGHT
1,800
rounds
per minute
cannon
can shoot
57,415 FEET (17,500 m)
MAXIMUM HEIGHT IT CAN FLY

Powerful Fighter

Experts think the MiG-35 will change warfare in the air. This speedy fighter will soon enter service. It will likely be a top fighter for years to come.

GLOSSARY

altitude (AL-ti-tood)—how high a place is above sea level or Earth's surface

barrel roll (BA-ruhl ROL)—a move in which a plane turns in a circle sideways while flying forward

cannon (KAN-uhn)—a large, heavy gun that fires explosives

detect (dee-TEKT)—to discover the existence or presence of something

dogfight (DAWG-fiyt)—a mid-air battle between fighter planes

missile (MIS-uhl)—a weapon that can be thrown or projected to hit an object far away

radar (RAY-dar)—a device that sends out radio waves for finding the location and speed of a moving object

stealth (STELTH)—an aircraft design that is hard for radar to pick up

LEARN MORE

BOOKS

Kennedy, Robert. *Would You Dare Fly a Fighter Jet?* Would You Dare? New York: Gareth Stevens, 2017.

Murray, Laura K. *Fighter Jets.* Seedlings. Mankato, MN: Creative Education and Creative Paperbacks, 2016.

Willis, John. *Fighter Jets.* Mighty Military Machines. New York: AV2 by Weigl, 2017.

WEBSITES

Meet the MiG-35
www.youtube.com/watch?v=jMZcRKGGTBc

MiG-35 Media
www.migavia.ru/index.php/en/gallery/category/23-mig-35

Military Aircraft
www.dkfindout.com/us/transportation/history-aircraft/military-aircraft/

INDEX